TREASURED JOURNALING MOMENTS

Copyright @ 2024 by Sandra W. Smith

All rights reserved.
This book or any portion thereof may not be reproduced or used in any manner whatsoever without written permission.

Printed in the United States of America by SCSXpressions.

LCCN 2024917061

For

Those seeking to capture a breath of joy and peace, behold a touch of beauty and grace in nature, prompting engaging journaling moments.

To

Charlandra, Sanitra and Caneara
Sons-in-love
Michael, Faith, Olivia, Parker, and Peyton
and
in honor of my parents, Wilbert Sr. and Susie

IN THE MORNING, O LORD, YOU HEAR MY VOICE; IN THE MORNING I LAY MY REQUEST BEFORE YOU AND WAIT IN EXPECTATION.

Psalm 5:3

Flowers touch our lives in many ways, like having a best friend who's always present. The aesthetic appeal, vibrant infused colors, and enchanting fragrances inspire calming effects that radiate peaceful moments of joy and often minimize stress. They are bright spots in our offices, uplift our spirits, are a beauty of elegance in our gardens, are radiant companions in our homes, an intricate part of a special ceremony, an umbrella of cheer for the sick, a staple of jubilance for the soon to be wed couple, the precious gift for the joyous new parents, and simply a splash of exuberance as a pick me up.

I've always been enamored with their delicacy and power. They evoke many emotions, sometimes prompting gregarious smiles, tears of joy, and a beaming heart filled with excitement. Flowers are undeniable blessings, to say the least. They have served numerous purposes from the earliest existence of time up to the present. They communicate love at congratulatory events, uttered as tokens of appreciation, an intricate part of a special celebration, the highlighting of a marked achievement, or simply the display of affection for a new beginning.

JOURNALING

Journaling has been a reliable companion that always seemed to be with me at every twist and turn of my life. Being a somewhat shy child and reserved by design, I learned early on that I was most at peace expressing myself on paper as well as inspiring others through some form of writing whether it was penning a special note on a notecard, composing an inspirational greeting, etching my thoughts on paper, or sending an encouraging message of cheer.

As you hold and read this special book, it is my prayer that you'll be inspired knowing this was written for you with love and sincere devotion.

HAVE A TREASURED JOURNALING EXPERIENCE.

SANDRA

TO GET THE MOST OUT OF YOUR JOURNALING EXPERIENCE:

- *Use the prompts to spark ideas, to encourage deeper reflection and for self-awareness.*

- *Create a peaceful, comfortable space free from distractions.*

- *Let your thoughts flow freely; don't worry about grammar or being perfect.*

- *Use a variety of formats: bullet points, sentences, or phrases - whatever feels right.*

- *Embrace the journey of growth and self-discovery.*

- *Relax, be open, and express yourself freely.*

- *Utilize the NOTE section at the end of the book to capture insights, expand ideas, reflect and revisit past entries.*

HE LOVES RIGHTEOUSNESS AND JUSTICE; THE EARTH IS FULL OF THE STEADFAST LOVE OF THE LORD.

Psalm 33:5

A flower's astounding color and peculiar shape, as well as the meaningful nourishment of love and gratitude, aid in keeping us connected to our almighty Creator who manifests and showers His love for mankind through his majestic and breathtaking handiwork surrounding us in nature. The spectacular beauty and comfort of a flower is a steady ray of sunshine.

THE HEAVENS DECLARE THE GLORY OF GOD, AND THE SKY ABOVE PROCLAIMS HIS HANDIWORK.

Psalm 19:1

JOURNALING PROMPT IDEAS:

THIS MORNING I FEEL
- AT PEACE
- BLESSED
- JOYFUL

MY GOALS FOR THE DAY
- TO PACE MYSELF
- TO WALK IN MY PURPOSE
- TO BE MORE PRAYERFUL

TODAY I'M GRATEFUL FOR
- MY FAMILY, CHILDREN AND GRANDCHILDREN
- ALL MY BLESSINGS
- MY HEALTH AND STRENGTH

TODAY I'M PRAYING FOR
- WORLD PEACE
- WISDOM IN DECISION-MAKING
- MY LOVED ONES AND FRIENDS WHO ARE ILL

JOURNALING PROMPT IDEAS CONT'D:

PROGRESS OR ACCOMPLISHMENTS I'VE MADE

I'M ECSTATIC I HAVE ACCOMPLISHED THE TASKS I SET OUT TO DO BY STAYING ON TRACK, PACING MYSELF, AND BEING MORE INTENTIONAL.

MY JOURNALING THOUGHTS FOR THE DAY

I'M SO THANKFUL I'M LEARNING TO EMBRACE PEACE MORE IN MY LIFE BY APPRECIATING THE SMALL THINGS. BEING MORE MINDFUL IN MY DAILY ACTIVITIES BRINGS A SENSE OF JOY AND TRANQUILITY. IT'S WONDERFUL TO KNOW THAT I DON'T HAVE TO BE CONSTANTLY BUSY. I'M GIVING MYSELF PERMISSION TO SLOW DOWN, RELAX, AND ENJOY THE JOURNEY.

I CHERISH GOD AND HIS MAJESTIC POWER AS I BEHOLD HIS BREATH TAKING CREATION.

CELESTIAL WONDERS

The abundance and magnificence of heaven are shared with mankind, forever connecting us to our loving Savior. God's artistry and power are ever-present, seen in sunbeams streaming from above, through towering trees, vibrant flowers, and illuminating twinkling stars that guide us at night.

An immeasurable testament of our majestic creator's presence is reflected in nature. Rather walking outdoors, feeling the gentle breeze, admiring the plentiful peaceful shores, witnessing an amazing sunrise, or marveling at God's pervasive creation, we are compelled to praise and thank Him for His omnipotent glory graciously showered upon us.

THIS MORNING I FEEL...

_____
_____
_____
_____

MY GOAL/S FOR TODAY...

_____
_____
_____
_____

TODAY I AM GRATEFUL FOR...

_____
_____
_____
_____

TODAY I'M PRAYING FOR...

_____
_____
_____
_____

PROGRESS OR ACCOMPLISHMENT I MADE TODAY...

_____
_____
_____
_____
_____
_____
_____
_____

MY JOURNALING THOUGHT FOR TODAY...

_____
_____
_____
_____
_____
_____
_____
_____
_____
_____
_____
_____
_____
_____
_____

✧ I RELISH GOD'S RIVETING ARTISTRY OF
BOUNTIFUL LOVE PERVASIVE ALL AROUND ME.

THIS MORNING I FEEL...

_____
_____
_____
_____
_____

MY GOAL/S FOR TODAY...

_____
_____
_____
_____
_____

TODAY I AM GRATEFUL FOR...

_____
_____
_____
_____
_____

TODAY I'M PRAYING FOR...

_____
_____
_____
_____

PROGRESS OR ACCOMPLISHMENT I MADE TODAY...

_____
_____
_____
_____
_____
_____
_____

MY JOURNALING THOUGHT FOR TODAY...

_____
_____
_____
_____
_____
_____
_____
_____
_____
_____
_____
_____
_____
_____
_____

✦ OCEANS, LAKES, RIVERS AND SEAS ARE CONSOLING, PEACEFUL SHORES OF ENDEARMENT. ✦

THIS MORNING I FEEL…

_____
_____
_____
_____
_____

MY GOAL/S FOR TODAY…

_____
_____
_____
_____
_____

TODAY I AM GRATEFUL FOR…

_____
_____
_____
_____
_____

TODAY I'M PRAYING FOR…

_____
_____
_____
_____

PROGRESS OR ACCOMPLISHMENT I MADE TODAY...

_____
_____
_____
_____
_____
_____
_____

MY JOURNALING THOUGHT FOR TODAY...

_____
_____
_____
_____
_____
_____
_____
_____
_____
_____
_____
_____
_____
_____

ILLUSTRIOUS SUNBEAMS OF HOPE PEEK THROUGH EXPANSIVE WINDOWS EXTENDING SHIMMERING RAYS OF STEADFAST ENDURANCE.

THIS MORNING I FEEL...

_____
_____
_____
_____
_____

MY GOAL/S FOR TODAY...

_____
_____
_____
_____
_____

TODAY I AM GRATEFUL FOR...

_____
_____
_____
_____
_____

TODAY I'M PRAYING FOR...

_____
_____
_____
_____
_____

PROGRESS OR ACCOMPLISHMENT I MADE TODAY...

_____
_____
_____
_____
_____
_____
_____

MY JOURNALING THOUGHT FOR TODAY...

_____
_____
_____
_____
_____
_____
_____
_____
_____
_____
_____
_____
_____
_____

✧ HUMBLED BY YOUR RAINBOW OF LOVE, LORD, TEACH ME TO
EARNESTLY PRAY AND ALIGN MY WILL WITH YOURS. ✧

HAVE AN INTENTIONAL DAY

MY POWER THOUGHT FOR THE DAY:

_____

_____

SCRIPTURE TO KEEP ME MINDFUL:

_____

_____

I'M BEING INTENTIONAL ABOUT…

_____

_____

I'M INCORPORATING JOY IN MY LIFE…

_____

_____

WHAT I'M DOING TO DEEPEN MY RELATIONSHIP WITH GOD:

- _____
- _____
- _____

WAYS I'M PURSUING PEACE:

_____

_____

_____

MY PRAYER FOR TODAY

_____
_____
_____

WHAT INSPIRED ME THIS WEEK

_____
_____
_____

GOD IS GOOD BECAUSE….

_____
_____
_____

I SEEK TO INSPIRE OTHERS BY:

_____
_____
_____

TO KEEP ME ENCOURAGED I:

_____
_____
_____

WHEN I WALK OUTSIDE AND OBSERVE NATURE, I FEEL…

_____
_____
_____

THIS MORNING I FEEL...

_____
_____
_____
_____

MY GOAL/S FOR TODAY...

_____
_____
_____
_____

TODAY I AM GRATEFUL FOR...

_____
_____
_____
_____

TODAY I'M PRAYING FOR...

_____
_____
_____
_____

PROGRESS OR ACCOMPLISHMENT I MADE TODAY...

_____
_____
_____
_____
_____
_____
_____
_____

MY JOURNALING THOUGHT FOR TODAY...

_____
_____
_____
_____
_____
_____
_____
_____
_____
_____
_____
_____
_____
_____
_____
_____
_____

✦ AS I CONSCIOUSLY SIT SPELLBOUND BY THE TRANQUIL OCEAN OF LOVE, I OVERWHELMINGLY CAPTURE GOD'S ABUNDANT POWER. ✦

THIS MORNING I FEEL...

_____
_____
_____
_____
_____

MY GOAL/S FOR TODAY...

_____
_____
_____
_____
_____

TODAY I AM GRATEFUL FOR...

_____
_____
_____
_____
_____

TODAY I'M PRAYING FOR...

_____
_____
_____
_____
_____

PROGRESS OR ACCOMPLISHMENT I MADE TODAY...

_____
_____
_____
_____
_____
_____
_____
_____

MY JOURNALING THOUGHT FOR TODAY...

_____
_____
_____
_____
_____
_____
_____
_____
_____
_____
_____
_____
_____
_____
_____
_____

✧ THE ENDEARING SMILE OF NATURE AMPLIFIES GOD'S ENRICHING HANDIWORK AND IMMEASURABLE FAITHFULNESS. ✧

THIS MORNING I FEEL...

_____
_____
_____
_____
_____

MY GOAL/S FOR TODAY...

_____
_____
_____
_____
_____

TODAY I AM GRATEFUL FOR...

_____
_____
_____
_____
_____

TODAY I'M PRAYING FOR...

_____
_____
_____
_____
_____

PROGRESS OR ACCOMPLISHMENT I MADE TODAY...

_____
_____
_____
_____
_____
_____
_____
_____

MY JOURNALING THOUGHT FOR TODAY...

_____
_____
_____
_____
_____
_____
_____
_____
_____
_____
_____
_____
_____
_____
_____
_____

"GOD'S OMNIPOTENT AND GLORIOUS CREATION IS A NURTURING HAND OF ASSURANCE AND PEACE."

THIS MORNING I FEEL...

_____
_____
_____
_____

MY GOAL/S FOR TODAY...

_____
_____
_____
_____

TODAY I AM GRATEFUL FOR...

_____
_____
_____
_____

TODAY I'M PRAYING FOR...

_____
_____
_____
_____

PROGRESS OR ACCOMPLISHMENT I MADE TODAY...

_____
_____
_____
_____
_____
_____
_____
_____
_____

MY JOURNALING THOUGHT FOR TODAY...

_____
_____
_____
_____
_____
_____
_____
_____
_____
_____
_____
_____
_____
_____
_____
_____

✦ FLUFFY CLOUDS OF DISCOVERY BESTOW RESOUNDING AWARENESS AND INDISPENSABLE ENCOURAGEMENT THROUGHOUT LIFE'S JOURNEY. ✦

THIS MORNING I FEEL...

_____
_____
_____
_____
_____

MY GOAL/S FOR TODAY...

_____
_____
_____
_____
_____

TODAY I AM GRATEFUL FOR...

_____
_____
_____
_____
_____

TODAY I'M PRAYING FOR...

_____
_____
_____
_____

PROGRESS OR ACCOMPLISHMENT I MADE TODAY...

_____
_____
_____
_____
_____
_____
_____

MY JOURNALING THOUGHT FOR TODAY...

_____
_____
_____
_____
_____
_____
_____
_____
_____
_____
_____
_____
_____
_____
_____
_____

GOD'S MIRACULOUS, ILLUSTRATED CREATION
MAGNIFIES HIS UNVEILING POWER AND MAGNIFICENT GLORY.

HAVE AN INTENTIONAL DAY

MY POWER THOUGHT FOR THE DAY:

_____

_____

SCRIPTURE TO KEEP ME MINDFUL:

_____

_____

I'M BEING INTENTIONAL ABOUT...

_____

_____

I'M INCORPORATING JOY IN MY LIFE...

_____

_____

WHAT I'M DOING TO DEEPEN MY RELATIONSHIP WITH GOD:

- _____
- _____
- _____

WAYS I'M PURSUING PEACE:

_____

_____

_____

MY PRAYER FOR TODAY

_____

_____

_____

WHAT INSPIRED ME THIS WEEK

_____

_____

_____

GOD IS GOOD BECAUSE….

_____

_____

_____

I SEEK TO INSPIRE OTHERS BY:

_____

_____

_____

TO KEEP ME ENCOURAGED I:

_____

_____

_____

WHEN I WALK OUTSIDE AND OBSERVE NATURE, I FEEL…

_____

_____

_____

THIS MORNING I FEEL...

_____
_____
_____
_____
_____

MY GOAL/S FOR TODAY...

_____
_____
_____
_____
_____

TODAY I AM GRATEFUL FOR...

_____
_____
_____
_____
_____

TODAY I'M PRAYING FOR...

_____
_____
_____
_____
_____

PROGRESS OR ACCOMPLISHMENT I MADE TODAY...

_____
_____
_____
_____
_____
_____
_____
_____

MY JOURNALING THOUGHT FOR TODAY...

_____
_____
_____
_____
_____
_____
_____
_____
_____
_____
_____
_____
_____
_____
_____
_____

YOU ARE COMPASSIONATELY ADORNED
AND GRACED WITH GOD'S UNCONDITIONAL GIFT OF LOVE.

THIS MORNING I FEEL...

_____
_____
_____
_____
_____

MY GOAL/S FOR TODAY...

_____
_____
_____
_____
_____

TODAY I AM GRATEFUL FOR...

_____
_____
_____
_____
_____

TODAY I'M PRAYING FOR...

_____
_____
_____
_____
_____

PROGRESS OR ACCOMPLISHMENT I MADE TODAY...

_____
_____
_____
_____
_____
_____
_____

MY JOURNALING THOUGHT FOR TODAY...

_____
_____
_____
_____
_____
_____
_____
_____
_____
_____
_____
_____
_____
_____

A TRANQUIL GLIMPSE OF HEAVEN'S ILLUMINATING LIGHT REFLECTS DESIGNED PURPOSE AND TRIUMPHANT VICTORY.

THIS MORNING I FEEL...

_____
_____
_____
_____
_____

MY GOAL/S FOR TODAY...

_____
_____
_____
_____
_____

TODAY I AM GRATEFUL FOR...

_____
_____
_____
_____
_____

TODAY I'M PRAYING FOR...

_____
_____
_____
_____
_____

PROGRESS OR ACCOMPLISHMENT I MADE TODAY...

_____
_____
_____
_____
_____
_____
_____
_____

MY JOURNALING THOUGHT FOR TODAY...

_____
_____
_____
_____
_____
_____
_____
_____
_____
_____
_____
_____
_____
_____
_____
_____

✦ THE PREVALENCE OF GOD'S MAJESTIC CREATION GREETS ME WITH AUDACIOUS GRANDEUR AND PROMISE, PROPELLING ME TO REJOICE IN EXPECTATION. ✦

THIS MORNING I FEEL...

_____
_____
_____
_____
_____

MY GOAL/S FOR TODAY...

_____
_____
_____
_____
_____

TODAY I AM GRATEFUL FOR...

_____
_____
_____
_____
_____

TODAY I'M PRAYING FOR...

_____
_____
_____
_____
_____

PROGRESS OR ACCOMPLISHMENT I MADE TODAY...

_____
_____
_____
_____
_____
_____
_____

MY JOURNALING THOUGHT FOR TODAY...

_____
_____
_____
_____
_____
_____
_____
_____
_____
_____
_____
_____
_____
_____

✦ GOD'S ENCHANTING WORKMANSHIP OF SPLENDOR PROFOUNDLY EASES MY FEARS, LOVINGLY GUIDING ME WITH MURALS OF PREVAILING FAITH. ✦

THIS MORNING I FEEL...

_____
_____
_____
_____
_____

MY GOAL/S FOR TODAY...

_____
_____
_____
_____
_____

TODAY I AM GRATEFUL FOR...

_____
_____
_____
_____
_____

TODAY I'M PRAYING FOR...

_____
_____
_____
_____
_____

PROGRESS OR ACCOMPLISHMENT I MADE TODAY...

_____
_____
_____
_____
_____
_____
_____

MY JOURNALING THOUGHT FOR TODAY...

_____
_____
_____
_____
_____
_____
_____
_____
_____
_____
_____
_____
_____
_____

THE EXALTED CANVAS OF CELESTIAL BEAUTY BIRTH
HARMONIOUS MELODIES OF GLEAMING HOPE.

HAVE AN INTENTIONAL DAY

MY POWER THOUGHT FOR THE DAY:

_____

_____

SCRIPTURE TO KEEP ME MINDFUL:

_____

_____

I'M BEING INTENTIONAL ABOUT...

_____

_____

I'M INCORPORATING JOY IN MY LIFE...

_____

_____

WHAT I'M DOING TO DEEPEN MY RELATIONSHIP WITH GOD:

- _____
- _____
- _____

WAYS I'M PURSUING PEACE:

_____

_____

_____

MY PRAYER FOR TODAY

_____

_____

_____

WHAT INSPIRED ME THIS WEEK

_____

_____

_____

GOD IS GOOD BECAUSE….

_____

_____

_____

I SEEK TO INSPIRE OTHERS BY:

_____

_____

_____

TO KEEP ME ENCOURAGED I:

_____

_____

_____

WHEN I WALK OUTSIDE AND OBSERVE NATURE, I FEEL…

_____

_____

_____

THIS MORNING I FEEL...

_____
_____
_____
_____
_____

MY GOAL/S FOR TODAY...

_____
_____
_____
_____
_____

TODAY I AM GRATEFUL FOR...

_____
_____
_____
_____
_____

TODAY I'M PRAYING FOR...

_____
_____
_____
_____
_____

PROGRESS OR ACCOMPLISHMENT I MADE TODAY...

_____
_____
_____
_____
_____
_____
_____
_____

MY JOURNALING THOUGHT FOR TODAY...

_____
_____
_____
_____
_____
_____
_____
_____
_____
_____
_____
_____
_____
_____
_____
_____

✦ LUMINOUS STARS GLISTEN EVER SO BRIGHT,
RELEASING ALTITUDES OF EXUBERANT JOY BEYOND MEASURE. ✦

THIS MORNING I FEEL...

_____
_____
_____
_____
_____

MY GOAL/S FOR TODAY...

_____
_____
_____
_____
_____

TODAY I AM GRATEFUL FOR...

_____
_____
_____
_____
_____

TODAY I'M PRAYING FOR...

_____
_____
_____
_____
_____

PROGRESS OR ACCOMPLISHMENT I MADE TODAY...

_____
_____
_____
_____
_____
_____
_____
_____

MY JOURNALING THOUGHT FOR TODAY...

_____
_____
_____
_____
_____
_____
_____
_____
_____
_____
_____
_____
_____
_____
_____

THE BECKONING AND HARMONIOUS SHORES OF ACCEPTANCE REFRESHES MY RECEPTIVE HEART USHERING CONSOLING EMBRACE AND RESPECT.

THIS MORNING I FEEL...

_____
_____
_____
_____
_____

MY GOAL/S FOR TODAY...

_____
_____
_____
_____
_____

TODAY I AM GRATEFUL FOR...

_____
_____
_____
_____
_____

TODAY I'M PRAYING FOR...

_____
_____
_____
_____

PROGRESS OR ACCOMPLISHMENT I MADE TODAY...

_____
_____
_____
_____
_____
_____
_____

MY JOURNALING THOUGHT FOR TODAY...

_____
_____
_____
_____
_____
_____
_____
_____
_____
_____
_____
_____
_____
_____

INSPIRING FLOWING RIVERS CASCADE
CONSOLING AND PEACEFUL HUGS OF CHEER.

THIS MORNING I FEEL...

_____
_____
_____
_____
_____

MY GOAL/S FOR TODAY...

_____
_____
_____
_____
_____

TODAY I AM GRATEFUL FOR...

_____
_____
_____
_____
_____

TODAY I'M PRAYING FOR...

_____
_____
_____
_____
_____

PROGRESS OR ACCOMPLISHMENT I MADE TODAY...

_____
_____
_____
_____
_____
_____
_____
_____

MY JOURNALING THOUGHT FOR TODAY...

_____
_____
_____
_____
_____
_____
_____
_____
_____
_____
_____
_____
_____
_____
_____

✦ HUMBLY BASKING IN AN OCEAN OF
UNCONDITIONAL LOVE IS A FOUNTAIN OF LIBERATING JOY. ✦

THIS MORNING I FEEL...

_____
_____
_____
_____

MY GOAL/S FOR TODAY...

_____
_____
_____
_____

TODAY I AM GRATEFUL FOR...

_____
_____
_____
_____

TODAY I'M PRAYING FOR...

_____
_____
_____
_____

PROGRESS OR ACCOMPLISHMENT I MADE TODAY...

_____
_____
_____
_____
_____
_____
_____

MY JOURNALING THOUGHT FOR TODAY...

_____
_____
_____
_____
_____
_____
_____
_____
_____
_____
_____
_____
_____
_____

THE REFRESHING WHISPERS OF THE SEA EMIT SOOTHING PLEASANTRIES OF SOLACE, CONFERRING TRIUMPHANT STRENGTH AND ASSURANCE.

HAVE AN INTENTIONAL DAY

MY POWER THOUGHT FOR THE DAY:

_____

_____

SCRIPTURE TO KEEP ME MINDFUL:

_____

_____

I'M BEING INTENTIONAL ABOUT…

_____

_____

I'M INCORPORATING JOY IN MY LIFE…

_____

_____

WHAT I'M DOING TO DEEPEN MY RELATIONSHIP WITH GOD:

- _____
- _____
- _____

WAYS I'M PURSUING PEACE:

_____

_____

_____

MY PRAYER FOR TODAY

_____
_____
_____

WHAT INSPIRED ME THIS WEEK

_____
_____
_____

GOD IS GOOD BECAUSE....

_____
_____
_____

I SEEK TO INSPIRE OTHERS BY:

_____
_____
_____

TO KEEP ME ENCOURAGED I:

_____
_____
_____

WHEN I WALK OUTSIDE AND OBSERVE NATURE, I FEEL...

_____
_____
_____

THIS MORNING I FEEL...

_____
_____
_____
_____

MY GOAL/S FOR TODAY...

_____
_____
_____
_____

TODAY I AM GRATEFUL FOR...

_____
_____
_____
_____

TODAY I'M PRAYING FOR...

_____
_____
_____
_____

PROGRESS OR ACCOMPLISHMENT I MADE TODAY...

_____
_____
_____
_____
_____
_____
_____

MY JOURNALING THOUGHT FOR TODAY...

_____
_____
_____
_____
_____
_____
_____
_____
_____
_____
_____
_____
_____
_____

✦ BREATHTAKING STREAMS OF ABUNDANCE AFFECTIONATELY SALUTE THE ENTHRALLING AND PROMINENT LORDSHIP OF OUR MIGHTY GOD. ✦

THIS MORNING I FEEL...

_____
_____
_____
_____
_____

MY GOAL/S FOR TODAY...

_____
_____
_____
_____
_____

TODAY I AM GRATEFUL FOR...

_____
_____
_____
_____
_____

TODAY I'M PRAYING FOR...

_____
_____
_____
_____
_____

PROGRESS OR ACCOMPLISHMENT I MADE TODAY...

_____
_____
_____
_____
_____
_____
_____

MY JOURNALING THOUGHT FOR TODAY...

_____
_____
_____
_____
_____
_____
_____
_____
_____
_____
_____
_____
_____
_____
_____

✧ WHAT A WONDER TO BEHOLD THE MESMERIZING AND BEAUTIFUL ORCHESTRA OF PICTURESQUE RIVERS. ✧

THIS MORNING I FEEL...

_____
_____
_____
_____
_____

MY GOAL/S FOR TODAY...

_____
_____
_____
_____
_____

TODAY I AM GRATEFUL FOR...

_____
_____
_____
_____
_____

TODAY I'M PRAYING FOR...

_____
_____
_____
_____
_____

PROGRESS OR ACCOMPLISHMENT I MADE TODAY...

_____
_____
_____
_____
_____
_____
_____

MY JOURNALING THOUGHT FOR TODAY...

_____
_____
_____
_____
_____
_____
_____
_____
_____
_____
_____
_____
_____
_____
_____

✦ HEAR THE GENTLE AND CONSOLING VOICE OF YESTERDAY'S SHORES
CONVEYING GOODNESS AND A PURPOSEFUL BEGINNING. ✦

THIS MORNING I FEEL...

_____
_____
_____
_____

MY GOAL/S FOR TODAY...

_____
_____
_____
_____

TODAY I AM GRATEFUL FOR...

_____
_____
_____
_____

TODAY I'M PRAYING FOR...

_____
_____
_____
_____

PROGRESS OR ACCOMPLISHMENT I MADE TODAY...

_____
_____
_____
_____
_____
_____
_____
_____

MY JOURNALING THOUGHT FOR TODAY...

_____
_____
_____
_____
_____
_____
_____
_____
_____
_____
_____
_____
_____
_____
_____

GOD'S PEACEFUL PRESENCE AFFECTIONATELY EASE MY CLIMATIC FEARS WITH NURTURING WAVES OF PREVALENT FAITH.

THIS MORNING I FEEL...

_____
_____
_____
_____
_____

MY GOAL/S FOR TODAY...

_____
_____
_____
_____
_____

TODAY I AM GRATEFUL FOR...

_____
_____
_____
_____
_____

TODAY I'M PRAYING FOR...

_____
_____
_____
_____
_____

PROGRESS OR ACCOMPLISHMENT I MADE TODAY...

_____
_____
_____
_____
_____
_____
_____
_____

MY JOURNALING THOUGHT FOR TODAY...

_____
_____
_____
_____
_____
_____
_____
_____
_____
_____
_____
_____
_____
_____
_____
_____

OCEANS OF LOVE CRY OUT, USHERING GENTLE WAVES
OF SOOTHING AFFECTION AND QUIET REASSURANCE.

HAVE AN INTENTIONAL DAY

MY POWER THOUGHT FOR THE DAY:

_____

_____

SCRIPTURE TO KEEP ME MINDFUL:

_____

_____

I'M BEING INTENTIONAL ABOUT…

_____

_____

I'M INCORPORATING JOY IN MY LIFE…

_____

_____

WHAT I'M DOING TO DEEPEN MY RELATIONSHIP WITH GOD:

- _____
- _____
- _____

WAYS I'M PURSUING PEACE:

_____

_____

_____

MY PRAYER FOR TODAY

_____
_____
_____

WHAT INSPIRED ME THIS WEEK

_____
_____
_____

GOD IS GOOD BECAUSE….

_____
_____
_____

I SEEK TO INSPIRE OTHERS BY:

_____
_____
_____

TO KEEP ME ENCOURAGED I:

_____
_____
_____

WHEN I WALK OUTSIDE AND OBSERVE NATURE, I FEEL…

_____
_____
_____

THIS MORNING I FEEL...

_____
_____
_____
_____
_____

MY GOAL/S FOR TODAY...

_____
_____
_____
_____
_____

TODAY I AM GRATEFUL FOR...

_____
_____
_____
_____
_____

TODAY I'M PRAYING FOR...

_____
_____
_____
_____
_____

PROGRESS OR ACCOMPLISHMENT I MADE TODAY...

_____
_____
_____
_____
_____
_____
_____

MY JOURNALING THOUGHT FOR TODAY...

_____
_____
_____
_____
_____
_____
_____
_____
_____
_____
_____
_____
_____
_____

THE COMPELLING STREAMS OF AFFIRMING TRUST
MANIFEST VICTORIOUS RIVERS OF FORTITUDE AND COURAGE.

THIS MORNING I FEEL...

_____
_____
_____
_____

MY GOAL/S FOR TODAY...

_____
_____
_____
_____
_____

TODAY I AM GRATEFUL FOR...

_____
_____
_____
_____

TODAY I'M PRAYING FOR...

_____
_____
_____
_____

PROGRESS OR ACCOMPLISHMENT I MADE TODAY...

_____
_____
_____
_____
_____
_____
_____
_____

MY JOURNALING THOUGHT FOR TODAY...

_____
_____
_____
_____
_____
_____
_____
_____
_____
_____
_____
_____
_____
_____
_____

✦ THE BEAUTIFUL, TRANQUIL RESERVOIR OF WISDOM,
BIRTH ENLIGHTENING SEAS OF CONFIDENCE. ✦

THIS MORNING I FEEL...

_____
_____
_____
_____

MY GOAL/S FOR TODAY...

_____
_____
_____
_____

TODAY I AM GRATEFUL FOR...

_____
_____
_____
_____

TODAY I'M PRAYING FOR...

_____
_____
_____
_____

PROGRESS OR ACCOMPLISHMENT I MADE TODAY...

_____
_____
_____
_____
_____
_____
_____

MY JOURNALING THOUGHT FOR TODAY...

_____
_____
_____
_____
_____
_____
_____
_____
_____
_____
_____
_____
_____
_____

*REFRESHING RIVERS OF CONSOLATION BESTOW
OVERFLOWING STREAMS OF TRANQUILITY.*

THIS MORNING I FEEL...

_____

_____

_____

_____

_____

MY GOAL/S FOR TODAY...

_____

_____

_____

_____

_____

TODAY I AM GRATEFUL FOR...

_____

_____

_____

_____

_____

TODAY I'M PRAYING FOR...

_____

_____

_____

_____

_____

PROGRESS OR ACCOMPLISHMENT I MADE TODAY...

_____
_____
_____
_____
_____
_____
_____
_____

MY JOURNALING THOUGHT FOR TODAY...

_____
_____
_____
_____
_____
_____
_____
_____
_____
_____
_____
_____
_____
_____
_____
_____

✦ THE MELODIOUS WAVES OF SWEET PEACE,
DISPENSES ANCHORED CONTENTMENT AND EXPANSIVE SOLITUDE. ✦

THIS MORNING I FEEL...

_____
_____
_____
_____
_____

MY GOAL/S FOR TODAY...

_____
_____
_____
_____
_____

TODAY I AM GRATEFUL FOR...

_____
_____
_____
_____
_____

TODAY I'M PRAYING FOR...

_____
_____
_____
_____
_____

PROGRESS OR ACCOMPLISHMENT I MADE TODAY...

_____
_____
_____
_____
_____
_____
_____

MY JOURNALING THOUGHT FOR TODAY...

_____
_____
_____
_____
_____
_____
_____
_____
_____
_____
_____
_____
_____
_____

✦ THE ROLLING TIDES OF LIFE EMIT PEACEFUL
WAVES OF IMMENSE BEAUTY. ✦

HAVE AN INTENTIONAL DAY

MY POWER THOUGHT FOR THE DAY:

_____

_____

SCRIPTURE TO KEEP ME MINDFUL:

_____

_____

I'M BEING INTENTIONAL ABOUT...

_____

_____

I'M INCORPORATING JOY IN MY LIFE...

_____

_____

WHAT I'M DOING TO DEEPEN MY RELATIONSHIP WITH GOD:

- _____
- _____
- _____

WAYS I'M PURSUING PEACE:

_____

_____

_____

MY PRAYER FOR TODAY

_____
_____
_____

WHAT INSPIRED ME THIS WEEK

_____
_____
_____

GOD IS GOOD BECAUSE….

_____
_____
_____

I SEEK TO INSPIRE OTHERS BY:

_____
_____
_____

TO KEEP ME ENCOURAGED I:

_____
_____
_____

WHEN I WALK OUTSIDE AND OBSERVE NATURE, I FEEL…

_____
_____
_____

THIS MORNING I FEEL...

_____
_____
_____
_____
_____

MY GOAL/S FOR TODAY...

_____
_____
_____
_____
_____

TODAY I AM GRATEFUL FOR...

_____
_____
_____
_____
_____

TODAY I'M PRAYING FOR...

_____
_____
_____
_____
_____

PROGRESS OR ACCOMPLISHMENT I MADE TODAY...

_____
_____
_____
_____
_____
_____
_____
_____

MY JOURNALING THOUGHT FOR TODAY...

_____
_____
_____
_____
_____
_____
_____
_____
_____
_____
_____
_____
_____
_____
_____

ENCHANTING FLOWERS OF COPIOUS STRENGTH
SURRENDER REFRESHING PETALS OF HOPE AND BOUNDLESS CHEER.

THIS MORNING I FEEL...

_____
_____
_____
_____
_____

MY GOAL/S FOR TODAY...

_____
_____
_____
_____
_____

TODAY I AM GRATEFUL FOR...

_____
_____
_____
_____

TODAY I'M PRAYING FOR...

_____
_____
_____
_____

PROGRESS OR ACCOMPLISHMENT I MADE TODAY...

_____
_____
_____
_____
_____
_____
_____
_____

MY JOURNALING THOUGHT FOR TODAY...

_____
_____
_____
_____
_____
_____
_____
_____
_____
_____
_____
_____
_____
_____
_____
_____
_____

YOUR VIBRANT COMPASSION REJUVENATES MY ACHING HEART, CATAPULTING PROMISE AND BLOSSOMING RENEWAL.

THIS MORNING I FEEL...

_____
_____
_____
_____
_____

MY GOAL/S FOR TODAY...

_____
_____
_____
_____
_____

TODAY I AM GRATEFUL FOR...

_____
_____
_____
_____
_____

TODAY I'M PRAYING FOR...

_____
_____
_____
_____
_____

PROGRESS OR ACCOMPLISHMENT I MADE TODAY...

_____
_____
_____
_____
_____
_____
_____

MY JOURNALING THOUGHT FOR TODAY...

_____
_____
_____
_____
_____
_____
_____
_____
_____
_____
_____
_____
_____
_____

CHERISHING YOUR INCREDULOUS SPLENDOR ACCELERATES FLOURISHING HEIGHTS OF IMMENSE GRATITUDE.

THIS MORNING I FEEL…

_____
_____
_____
_____
_____

MY GOAL/S FOR TODAY…

_____
_____
_____
_____
_____

TODAY I AM GRATEFUL FOR…

_____
_____
_____
_____
_____

TODAY I'M PRAYING FOR…

_____
_____
_____
_____
_____

PROGRESS OR ACCOMPLISHMENT I MADE TODAY...

_____
_____
_____
_____
_____
_____
_____

MY JOURNALING THOUGHT FOR TODAY...

_____
_____
_____
_____
_____
_____
_____
_____
_____
_____
_____
_____
_____
_____

GOD'S PEACEFUL PRESENCE OF EXUBERANT COLOR IS
A GARDEN OF INSURMOUNTABLE AND TRANSCENDING LOVE.

THIS MORNING I FEEL...

_____
_____
_____
_____
_____

MY GOAL/S FOR TODAY...

_____
_____
_____
_____
_____

TODAY I AM GRATEFUL FOR...

_____
_____
_____
_____
_____

TODAY I'M PRAYING FOR...

_____
_____
_____
_____
_____

PROGRESS OR ACCOMPLISHMENT I MADE TODAY...

_____
_____
_____
_____
_____
_____
_____

MY JOURNALING THOUGHT FOR TODAY...

_____
_____
_____
_____
_____
_____
_____
_____
_____
_____
_____
_____
_____
_____

✦ LORD, YOUR MAJESTIC CANOPY OF COUNTLESS COMPASSION
AND BLESSINGS CONFER RENEWED HOPE AND COMFORT. ✦

HAVE AN INTENTIONAL DAY

MY POWER THOUGHT FOR THE DAY:

_____

_____

SCRIPTURE TO KEEP ME MINDFUL:

_____

_____

I'M BEING INTENTIONAL ABOUT...

_____

_____

I'M INCORPORATING JOY IN MY LIFE...

_____

_____

WHAT I'M DOING TO DEEPEN MY RELATIONSHIP WITH GOD:

- _____
- _____
- _____

WAYS I'M PURSUING PEACE:

_____

_____

_____

MY PRAYER FOR TODAY

_____
_____
_____

WHAT INSPIRED ME THIS WEEK

_____
_____
_____

GOD IS GOOD BECAUSE....

_____
_____
_____

I SEEK TO INSPIRE OTHERS BY:

_____
_____
_____

TO KEEP ME ENCOURAGED I:

_____
_____
_____

WHEN I WALK OUTSIDE AND OBSERVE NATURE, I FEEL...

_____
_____
_____

THIS MORNING I FEEL...

_____
_____
_____
_____
_____

MY GOAL/S FOR TODAY...

_____
_____
_____
_____
_____

TODAY I AM GRATEFUL FOR...

_____
_____
_____
_____
_____

TODAY I'M PRAYING FOR...

_____
_____
_____
_____
_____

PROGRESS OR ACCOMPLISHMENT I MADE TODAY...

_____
_____
_____
_____
_____
_____
_____
_____

MY JOURNALING THOUGHT FOR TODAY...

_____
_____
_____
_____
_____
_____
_____
_____
_____
_____
_____
_____
_____
_____
_____
_____

THE ALLURING BEAUTY OF LIFE'S FLOURISHING FLOWERS USHER FAITH AND APPRECIATION, AFFIRMING I'M RESILIENT AND COMPLETE.

THIS MORNING I FEEL...

_____
_____
_____
_____
_____

MY GOAL/S FOR TODAY...

_____
_____
_____
_____
_____

TODAY I AM GRATEFUL FOR...

_____
_____
_____
_____
_____

TODAY I'M PRAYING FOR...

_____
_____
_____
_____
_____

PROGRESS OR ACCOMPLISHMENT I MADE TODAY...

_____
_____
_____
_____
_____
_____
_____
_____

MY JOURNALING THOUGHT FOR TODAY...

_____
_____
_____
_____
_____
_____
_____
_____
_____
_____
_____
_____
_____
_____
_____
_____

YOUR DELICATE AND EXQUISITE PETALS OF STRENGTH PROMENADE PEACEFUL ENERGIES OF PURPOSE AND STILLNESS.

THIS MORNING I FEEL...

_____
_____
_____
_____

MY GOAL/S FOR TODAY...

_____
_____
_____
_____

TODAY I AM GRATEFUL FOR...

_____
_____
_____
_____

TODAY I'M PRAYING FOR...

_____
_____
_____
_____

PROGRESS OR ACCOMPLISHMENT I MADE TODAY...

_____
_____
_____
_____
_____
_____
_____
_____

MY JOURNALING THOUGHT FOR TODAY...

_____
_____
_____
_____
_____
_____
_____
_____
_____
_____
_____
_____
_____
_____
_____
_____
_____

✦ FOREVER INSPIRED BY AWAKENING FLOWERS
OF RADIANT DELIGHT AND BENEVOLENT AFFECTION. ✦

THIS MORNING I FEEL...

_____
_____
_____
_____
_____

MY GOAL/S FOR TODAY...

_____
_____
_____
_____
_____

TODAY I AM GRATEFUL FOR...

_____
_____
_____
_____
_____

TODAY I'M PRAYING FOR...

_____
_____
_____
_____
_____

PROGRESS OR ACCOMPLISHMENT I MADE TODAY...

_____
_____
_____
_____
_____
_____

MY JOURNALING THOUGHT FOR TODAY...

_____
_____
_____
_____
_____
_____
_____
_____
_____
_____
_____
_____

✧ AS YOU GRACEFULLY EXTEND YOUR RECEPTIVE ARMS,
I INSTANTANEOUSLY FEEL THE GARNISHING EMBRACE OF VICTORY. ✧

THIS MORNING I FEEL...

_____
_____
_____
_____
_____

MY GOAL/S FOR TODAY...

_____
_____
_____
_____
_____

TODAY I AM GRATEFUL FOR...

_____
_____
_____
_____
_____

TODAY I'M PRAYING FOR...

_____
_____
_____
_____
_____

PROGRESS OR ACCOMPLISHMENT I MADE TODAY...

_____
_____
_____
_____
_____
_____
_____
_____

MY JOURNALING THOUGHT FOR TODAY...

_____
_____
_____
_____
_____
_____
_____
_____
_____
_____
_____
_____
_____
_____
_____
_____

✦ YOUR DEBONAIR PRESENCE OF BEAUTY FOSTERS
CASCADING COLORS OF CONFIDENCE AND HUMILITY. ✦

HAVE AN INTENTIONAL DAY

MY POWER THOUGHT FOR THE DAY:

_____

_____

SCRIPTURE TO KEEP ME MINDFUL:

_____

_____

I'M BEING INTENTIONAL ABOUT...

_____

_____

I'M INCORPORATING JOY IN MY LIFE...

_____

_____

WHAT I'M DOING TO DEEPEN MY RELATIONSHIP WITH GOD:

- _____
- _____
- _____

WAYS I'M PURSUING PEACE:

_____

_____

_____

MY PRAYER FOR TODAY

_____
_____
_____

WHAT INSPIRED ME THIS WEEK

_____
_____
_____

GOD IS GOOD BECAUSE....

_____
_____
_____

I SEEK TO INSPIRE OTHERS BY:

_____
_____
_____

TO KEEP ME ENCOURAGED I:

_____
_____
_____

WHEN I WALK OUTSIDE AND OBSERVE NATURE, I FEEL...

_____
_____
_____

THIS MORNING I FEEL...

_____
_____
_____
_____

MY GOAL/S FOR TODAY...

_____
_____
_____
_____

TODAY I AM GRATEFUL FOR...

_____
_____
_____
_____

TODAY I'M PRAYING FOR...

_____
_____
_____
_____

PROGRESS OR ACCOMPLISHMENT I MADE TODAY...

_____
_____
_____
_____
_____
_____
_____

MY JOURNALING THOUGHT FOR TODAY...

_____
_____
_____
_____
_____
_____
_____
_____
_____
_____
_____
_____
_____
_____

✦ LIFE'S PROMENADING WHISPERS OF HOPE SERENADE
TULIPS OF CONTENTMENT AND FRAGRANT ASPIRATIONS. ✦

THIS MORNING I FEEL...

_____
_____
_____
_____
_____

MY GOAL/S FOR TODAY...

_____
_____
_____
_____
_____

TODAY I AM GRATEFUL FOR...

_____
_____
_____
_____
_____

TODAY I'M PRAYING FOR...

_____
_____
_____
_____
_____

PROGRESS OR ACCOMPLISHMENT I MADE TODAY...

_____
_____
_____
_____
_____
_____
_____

MY JOURNALING THOUGHT FOR TODAY...

_____
_____
_____
_____
_____
_____
_____
_____
_____
_____
_____
_____
_____
_____
_____

✦ THE BEAUTIFUL BLOSSOMING FLOWERS OF KINDNESS MAGNIFY
FRAGRANT AROMAS OF SELF-WORTH, AFFIRMING I AM ENOUGH. ✦

THIS MORNING I FEEL...

_____
_____
_____
_____
_____

MY GOAL/S FOR TODAY...

_____
_____
_____
_____
_____

TODAY I AM GRATEFUL FOR...

_____
_____
_____
_____
_____

TODAY I'M PRAYING FOR...

_____
_____
_____
_____
_____

PROGRESS OR ACCOMPLISHMENT I MADE TODAY...

_____
_____
_____
_____
_____
_____
_____
_____

MY JOURNALING THOUGHT FOR TODAY...

_____
_____
_____
_____
_____
_____
_____
_____
_____
_____
_____
_____
_____
_____
_____

✦ STRENGTHENING CHALLENGES NOURISH MY
SOUL WITH BOUNTIFUL BOUQUETS OF PROMISE. ✦

THIS MORNING I FEEL...

_____
_____
_____
_____

MY GOAL/S FOR TODAY...

_____
_____
_____
_____

TODAY I AM GRATEFUL FOR...

_____
_____
_____
_____

TODAY I'M PRAYING FOR...

_____
_____
_____
_____

PROGRESS OR ACCOMPLISHMENT I MADE TODAY...

_____
_____
_____
_____
_____
_____
_____
_____

MY JOURNALING THOUGHT FOR TODAY...

_____
_____
_____
_____
_____
_____
_____
_____
_____
_____
_____
_____
_____
_____
_____
_____

*KEEP SOARING TO DESTINED HEIGHTS
SWADDLED IN PASSIONATE FAITH AND FORTITUDE.*

THIS MORNING I FEEL...

_____
_____
_____
_____
_____

MY GOAL/S FOR TODAY...

_____
_____
_____
_____
_____

TODAY I AM GRATEFUL FOR...

_____
_____
_____
_____
_____

TODAY I'M PRAYING FOR...

_____
_____
_____
_____
_____

PROGRESS OR ACCOMPLISHMENT I MADE TODAY...

_____
_____
_____
_____
_____
_____
_____
_____

MY JOURNALING THOUGHT FOR TODAY...

_____
_____
_____
_____
_____
_____
_____
_____
_____
_____
_____
_____
_____
_____

OUR TREASURED AND UNBREAKABLE FRIENDSHIP'S AN UNCONDITIONAL OCEAN OF HARMONY.

HAVE AN INTENTIONAL DAY

MY POWER THOUGHT FOR THE DAY:

_____

_____

SCRIPTURE TO KEEP ME MINDFUL:

_____

_____

I'M BEING INTENTIONAL ABOUT...

_____

_____

I'M INCORPORATING JOY IN MY LIFE...

_____

_____

WHAT I'M DOING TO DEEPEN MY RELATIONSHIP WITH GOD:

- _____
- _____
- _____

WAYS I'M PURSUING PEACE:

_____

_____

_____

MY PRAYER FOR TODAY

_____

_____

_____

WHAT INSPIRED ME THIS WEEK

_____

_____

_____

GOD IS GOOD BECAUSE….

_____

_____

_____

I SEEK TO INSPIRE OTHERS BY:

_____

_____

_____

TO KEEP ME ENCOURAGED I:

_____

_____

_____

WHEN I WALK OUTSIDE AND OBSERVE NATURE, I FEEL…

_____

_____

_____

THIS MORNING I FEEL...

_____
_____
_____
_____

MY GOAL/S FOR TODAY...

_____
_____
_____
_____

TODAY I AM GRATEFUL FOR...

_____
_____
_____
_____

TODAY I'M PRAYING FOR...

_____
_____
_____
_____

PROGRESS OR ACCOMPLISHMENT I MADE TODAY...

_____
_____
_____
_____
_____
_____
_____

MY JOURNALING THOUGHT FOR TODAY...

_____
_____
_____
_____
_____
_____
_____
_____
_____
_____
_____
_____
_____
_____
_____

LIFE'S MOUNTAINOUS VALLEYS OF STRENGTH PRODUCE STABILIZING FORCES OF COMFORT.

THIS MORNING I FEEL...

_____
_____
_____
_____
_____

MY GOAL/S FOR TODAY...

_____
_____
_____
_____
_____

TODAY I AM GRATEFUL FOR...

_____
_____
_____
_____
_____

TODAY I'M PRAYING FOR...

_____
_____
_____
_____
_____

PROGRESS OR ACCOMPLISHMENT I MADE TODAY...

_____
_____
_____
_____
_____
_____
_____
_____

MY JOURNALING THOUGHT FOR TODAY...

_____
_____
_____
_____
_____
_____
_____
_____
_____
_____
_____
_____
_____
_____
_____

KEEP GROWING AND PREVAILING THROUGH LIFE'S UNCERTAINTIES WITH FEARLESS FAITH AND FERVENT PRAYER.

THIS MORNING I FEEL...

_____

_____

_____

_____

MY GOAL/S FOR TODAY...

_____

_____

_____

_____

TODAY I AM GRATEFUL FOR...

_____

_____

_____

_____

TODAY I'M PRAYING FOR...

_____

_____

_____

_____

PROGRESS OR ACCOMPLISHMENT I MADE TODAY...

_____
_____
_____
_____
_____
_____
_____
_____
_____

MY JOURNALING THOUGHT FOR TODAY...

_____
_____
_____
_____
_____
_____
_____
_____
_____
_____
_____
_____
_____
_____
_____
_____
_____

✧ ASCEND TO GOD ORDAINED HEIGHTS ANCHORED
IN JOYOUS RIVERS OF STEADFASTNESS. ✧

THIS MORNING I FEEL...

_____
_____
_____
_____

MY GOAL/S FOR TODAY...

_____
_____
_____
_____

TODAY I AM GRATEFUL FOR...

_____
_____
_____
_____

TODAY I'M PRAYING FOR...

_____
_____
_____
_____

PROGRESS OR ACCOMPLISHMENT I MADE TODAY...

_____
_____
_____
_____
_____
_____
_____

MY JOURNALING THOUGHT FOR TODAY...

_____
_____
_____
_____
_____
_____
_____
_____
_____
_____
_____
_____
_____
_____

I'M ENAMORED WITH GOD'S PREVAILING PRESENCE AND INDESCRIBABLE GOODNESS; I REVERE ALMIGHTY GOD.

THIS MORNING I FEEL...

MY GOAL/S FOR TODAY...

TODAY I AM GRATEFUL FOR...

TODAY I'M PRAYING FOR...

PROGRESS OR ACCOMPLISHMENT I MADE TODAY...

_____
_____
_____
_____
_____
_____
_____
_____

MY JOURNALING THOUGHT FOR TODAY...

_____
_____
_____
_____
_____
_____
_____
_____
_____
_____
_____
_____
_____
_____
_____
_____

THE GRATIFYING PETALS OF YESTERDAY ARE RIVETING RAINBOWS OF GREATNESS.

HAVE AN INTENTIONAL DAY

MY POWER THOUGHT FOR THE DAY:

_____

_____

SCRIPTURE TO KEEP ME MINDFUL:

_____

_____

I'M BEING INTENTIONAL ABOUT...

_____

_____

I'M INCORPORATING JOY IN MY LIFE...

_____

_____

WHAT I'M DOING TO DEEPEN MY RELATIONSHIP WITH GOD:

- _____
- _____
- _____

WAYS I'M PURSUING PEACE:

_____

_____

_____

MY PRAYER FOR TODAY

_____
_____
_____

WHAT INSPIRED ME THIS WEEK

_____
_____
_____

GOD IS GOOD BECAUSE….

_____
_____
_____

I SEEK TO INSPIRE OTHERS BY:

_____
_____
_____

TO KEEP ME ENCOURAGED I:

_____
_____
_____

WHEN I WALK OUTSIDE AND OBSERVE NATURE, I FEEL…

_____
_____
_____

THIS MORNING I FEEL...

_____
_____
_____
_____

MY GOAL/S FOR TODAY...

_____
_____
_____
_____

TODAY I AM GRATEFUL FOR...

_____
_____
_____
_____

TODAY I'M PRAYING FOR...

_____
_____
_____
_____

PROGRESS OR ACCOMPLISHMENT I MADE TODAY...

_____
_____
_____
_____
_____
_____
_____

MY JOURNALING THOUGHT FOR TODAY...

_____
_____
_____
_____
_____
_____
_____
_____
_____
_____
_____
_____
_____
_____

✧ MOUNTAINS OF FERVENT PRAYER ARE
ENCHANTING RESERVOIRS OF BLESSINGS. ✧

THIS MORNING I FEEL...

_____
_____
_____
_____
_____

MY GOAL/S FOR TODAY...

_____
_____
_____
_____
_____

TODAY I AM GRATEFUL FOR...

_____
_____
_____
_____
_____

TODAY I'M PRAYING FOR...

_____
_____
_____
_____

PROGRESS OR ACCOMPLISHMENT I MADE TODAY...

_____
_____
_____
_____
_____
_____
_____
_____

MY JOURNALING THOUGHT FOR TODAY...

_____
_____
_____
_____
_____
_____
_____
_____
_____
_____
_____
_____
_____

FLOWING WATERS OF STRENGTHENING TIDES ARE VIBRANT FRIENDSHIPS OF LOVE.

THIS MORNING I FEEL...

_____
_____
_____
_____
_____

MY GOAL/S FOR TODAY...

_____
_____
_____
_____
_____

TODAY I AM GRATEFUL FOR...

_____
_____
_____
_____
_____

TODAY I'M PRAYING FOR...

_____
_____
_____
_____
_____

PROGRESS OR ACCOMPLISHMENT I MADE TODAY...

_____
_____
_____
_____
_____
_____
_____
_____

MY JOURNALING THOUGHT FOR TODAY...

_____
_____
_____
_____
_____
_____
_____
_____
_____
_____
_____
_____
_____
_____
_____
_____

✧ MELODIOUS FRIENDSHIPS OF TRUST IS A
TREASURE CHEST OF PRICELESS JEWELS. ✧

THIS MORNING I FEEL...

_____
_____
_____
_____

MY GOAL/S FOR TODAY...

_____
_____
_____
_____

TODAY I AM GRATEFUL FOR...

_____
_____
_____
_____

TODAY I'M PRAYING FOR...

_____
_____
_____
_____

PROGRESS OR ACCOMPLISHMENT I MADE TODAY...

_____
_____
_____
_____
_____
_____
_____

MY JOURNALING THOUGHT FOR TODAY...

_____
_____
_____
_____
_____
_____
_____
_____
_____
_____
_____
_____
_____
_____

✦ REVERE THE GLORIOUS AND POWERFUL
TAPESTRY OF THE MASTER'S TOUCH. ✦

THIS MORNING I FEEL…

_____
_____
_____
_____

MY GOAL/S FOR TODAY…

_____
_____
_____
_____

TODAY I AM GRATEFUL FOR…

_____
_____
_____
_____

TODAY I'M PRAYING FOR…

_____
_____
_____
_____

PROGRESS OR ACCOMPLISHMENT I MADE TODAY...

_____
_____
_____
_____
_____
_____
_____
_____

MY JOURNALING THOUGHT FOR TODAY...

_____
_____
_____
_____
_____
_____
_____
_____
_____
_____
_____
_____
_____
_____
_____

BECKONING SHORES OF ACCEPTANCE,
REFRESH MY RECEPTIVE HEART WITH LOVING CARE.

HAVE AN INTENTIONAL DAY

MY POWER THOUGHT FOR THE DAY:

_____

_____

SCRIPTURE TO KEEP ME MINDFUL:

_____

_____

I'M BEING INTENTIONAL ABOUT...

_____

_____

I'M INCORPORATING JOY IN MY LIFE...

_____

_____

WHAT I'M DOING TO DEEPEN MY RELATIONSHIP WITH GOD:

- _____
- _____
- _____

WAYS I'M PURSUING PEACE:

_____

_____

_____

MY PRAYER FOR TODAY

_____

_____

_____

WHAT INSPIRED ME THIS WEEK

_____

_____

_____

GOD IS GOOD BECAUSE….

_____

_____

_____

I SEEK TO INSPIRE OTHERS BY:

_____

_____

_____

TO KEEP ME ENCOURAGED I:

_____

_____

_____

WHEN I WALK OUTSIDE AND OBSERVE NATURE, I FEEL…

_____

_____

_____

HAVE AN INTENTIONAL DAY

MY POWER THOUGHT FOR THE DAY:
_____
_____

SCRIPTURE TO KEEP ME MINDFUL:
_____
_____

I'M BEING INTENTIONAL ABOUT…
_____
_____

I'M INCORPORATING JOY IN MY LIFE…
_____
_____

WHAT I'M DOING TO DEEPEN MY RELATIONSHIP WITH GOD:
- _____
- _____
- _____

WAYS I'M PURSUING PEACE:
_____
_____
_____

MY PRAYER FOR TODAY

_____
_____
_____

WHAT INSPIRED ME THIS WEEK

_____
_____
_____

GOD IS GOOD BECAUSE….

_____
_____
_____

I SEEK TO INSPIRE OTHERS BY:

_____
_____
_____

TO KEEP ME ENCOURAGED I:

_____
_____
_____

WHEN I WALK OUTSIDE AND OBSERVE NATURE, I FEEL…

_____
_____
_____

HAVE AN INTENTIONAL DAY

MY POWER THOUGHT FOR THE DAY:
_____
_____

SCRIPTURE TO KEEP ME MINDFUL:
_____
_____

I'M BEING INTENTIONAL ABOUT...
_____
_____

I'M INCORPORATING JOY IN MY LIFE...
_____
_____

WHAT I'M DOING TO DEEPEN MY RELATIONSHIP WITH GOD:
- _____
- _____
- _____

WAYS I'M PURSUING PEACE:
_____
_____
_____

MY PRAYER FOR TODAY

_____

_____

_____

WHAT INSPIRED ME THIS WEEK

_____

_____

_____

GOD IS GOOD BECAUSE….

_____

_____

_____

I SEEK TO INSPIRE OTHERS BY:

_____

_____

_____

TO KEEP ME ENCOURAGED I:

_____

_____

_____

WHEN I WALK OUTSIDE AND OBSERVE NATURE, I FEEL…

_____

_____

_____

HAVE AN INTENTIONAL DAY

MY POWER THOUGHT FOR THE DAY:

_____

_____

SCRIPTURE TO KEEP ME MINDFUL:

_____

_____

I'M BEING INTENTIONAL ABOUT...

_____

_____

I'M INCORPORATING JOY IN MY LIFE...

_____

_____

WHAT I'M DOING TO DEEPEN MY RELATIONSHIP WITH GOD:

- _____
- _____
- _____

WAYS I'M PURSUING PEACE:

_____

_____

_____

MY PRAYER FOR TODAY

_____
_____
_____

WHAT INSPIRED ME THIS WEEK

_____
_____
_____

GOD IS GOOD BECAUSE….

_____
_____
_____

I SEEK TO INSPIRE OTHERS BY:

_____
_____
_____

TO KEEP ME ENCOURAGED I:

_____
_____
_____

WHEN I WALK OUTSIDE AND OBSERVE NATURE, I FEEL…

_____
_____
_____

NOTES

NOTES

NOTES

NOTES

NOTES

NOTES

NOTES

NOTES

NOTES

NOTES

THANK YOU so much for purchasing my book!

Please consider leaving a BOOK REVIEW.
Every review helps me reach more readers like you.

You can scan the QR code or use the provided link to share your thoughts.

SCAN QR CODE

LINK
https://amazon.com/author/sandra-xpressions.inspire

So Appreciative,
Sandra

www.ingramcontent.com/pod-product-compliance
Lightning Source LLC
LaVergne TN
LVHW052244070526
838201LV00094B/220